?
E
XTRA
ORDINARY

For Patator and all those kiddos with glasses that sometimes seem too big or too serious for their little round faces.

HELVETIQ publishing has been supported by the Swiss Federal Office of Culture with a structural grant for the years 2021-2025.

With the support of:

LOTERIE ROMANDE

Extraordinary Eyeglasses
The Amazing Invention That Helps Us See

Caroline Stevan, François Vigneault

Text: Caroline Stevan
Illustrations: François Vigneault
Optical illusion p. 74: Shutterstock.com - Perepadia Y
Layout: François Vigneault
Typesetting: Sarah Mühlebach
Editor: Richard Harvell
Proofreader: Karin Waldhauser

ISBN: 978-3-03964-026-3
First edition: August 2024
Deposit copy in the Library of Congress: 2024
Printed in the Czech Republic

Mittlere Strasse 4
CH-4056 Basel
Switzerland

HELVETIQ helvetiq.com

MIX
Paper from responsible sources
FSC® C014138

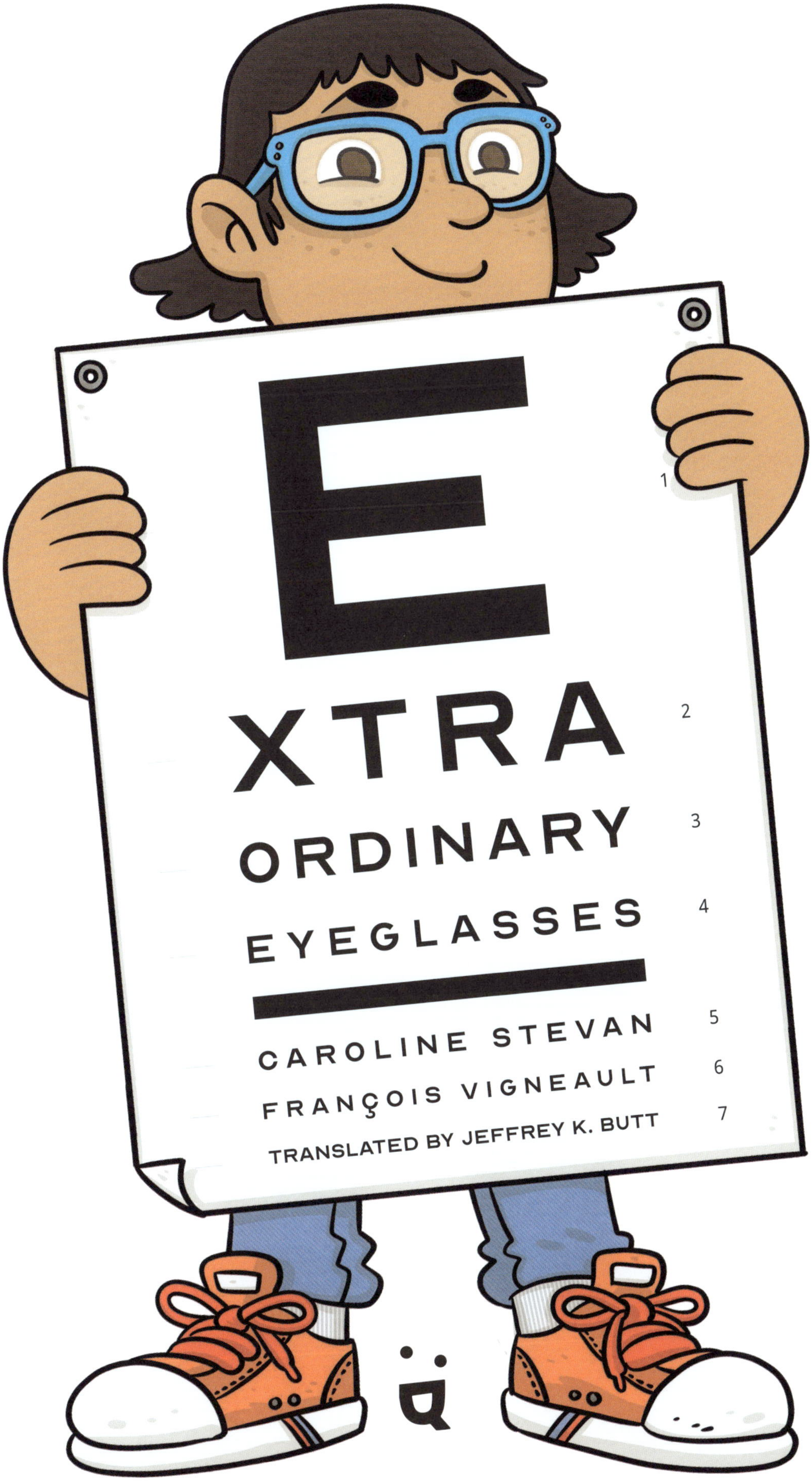
E
1
XTRA
2
ORDINARY
3
EYEGLASSES
4
CAROLINE STEVAN
5
FRANÇOIS VIGNEAULT
6
TRANSLATED BY JEFFREY K. BUTT
7

Extraordinary Eyeglasses

The Amazing Invention That Helps Us See

Dear Reader,
Do you wear glasses? If so, you're in luck because that means you can see things two different ways! When you have your glasses on, you can probably see like everyone else, but when you take them off, things get a little blurred or distorted. Give it a quick try! When I was little and just wanted to be left alone, I'd simply take my glasses off, and everyone just seemed to disappear. Suddenly, I was in my own little world. Superpowers should never be overused, so don't try to see without your glasses too often or else your eyes and head might start to ache ... But just knowing you have two ways to see the world, when a lot of people have only one, well that alone is pretty cool, isn't it?

2.2 billion

people in the world—about one in four—need glasses, but don't have them.

4.8 billion
people will be nearsighted by 2050, mostly because of all the time they spend staring at screens.

2nd Thursday of October
World Sight Day

9/10
In Japan, China, and South Korea, 9 out of every 10 students are already wearing glasses!

Glasses Around the World

Who Invented Glasses?

More than 2,000 years ago, **Roman emperor Nero** used an emerald-green stone as sunglasses so he could watch gladiators fight in an arena. Crazy, right?

We also know from old documents that people made magnifying glasses by filling glass bowls with water.

0 — 1200

In the 13th century, rock crystal was placed on the pages of books to enlarge the letters. Then someone had a lightbulb moment and instead put them directly in front of their eyes! Who came up with the idea? There are several theories—the Arabian Ibn al-Haytham, Englishman Roger Bacon, and Italians Luigi Zecchin, Sandro di Popozo, or Alessandro Spina. No matter who it was, glasses were born! Lots of eyeglasses would be made in Italy, where there was a history of working with glass, and the use of rock crystal was soon abandoned.

Because they were responsible for copying books, **monks** especially needed eyeglasses. That's right, back then, books were handprinted ... and sometimes they were thousands of pages long! With the invention of the printing press in Germany around 1450, books became more common ... and so did the need for eyeglasses.

No sooner were glasses invented than they began to turn up in paintings, just like in this portrait of a priest painted by the Italian Tommaso da Modena in 1352.

In the 17th century, various attempts were made to keep glasses from falling off, like tying them around the head with a ribbon or using a bar hidden under the hat.

In the 18th century, **opera glasses**, **monocles**, **scissors-glasses**, and **lorgnettes** began to appear. Since these accessories were made from precious materials, they came to be regarded as jewelry, sometimes with no actual medical purpose. Because of this, they were available only to the wealthiest, who used them for things like getting a better view of the stage at the theater.

In 1727, the **first frames** were designed by Englishman Edward Scarlett.
They don't look very comfortable, do they?!

In 1784, American **Benjamin Franklin** fashioned his own pair of glasses by joining two half-lenses to see things both up close and at a distance. These are called "bifocals."
Far vision
Near vision

In 1796, Pierre-Hyacinthe Caseaux, a nail maker from the Jura region of France, replaced the broken frame of his glasses with a **wire frame**.

These “hair glasses” or “wire glasses” were very light and revolutionized comfort. For the first time, eyeglasses were made in factories.

In the 19th century, lens production became more refined, allowing more and more vision problems to be corrected.

The end of the 19th century saw the invention of the first **contact lenses**, little glass disks placed directly on the eyes. At the time, they were heavy and very fragile, not to mention uncomfortable and dangerous to wear.

In 1938, American physicist **Katherine Blodgett** had the clever idea to invent nonreflective glass.

2000
In the 20th century, plastic was invented. Thanks to this material, soft lenses were introduced, and glasses began to appear in incredible shapes and colors.
They also became more affordable, and more and more people finally had access to glasses.
Turn the page!

WHICH ONES DO YOU PREFER?

Beryl
and the Superpowered Spectacles
?

AAAAAHH!!
?
AAAAH!
!
END

The Human Eye

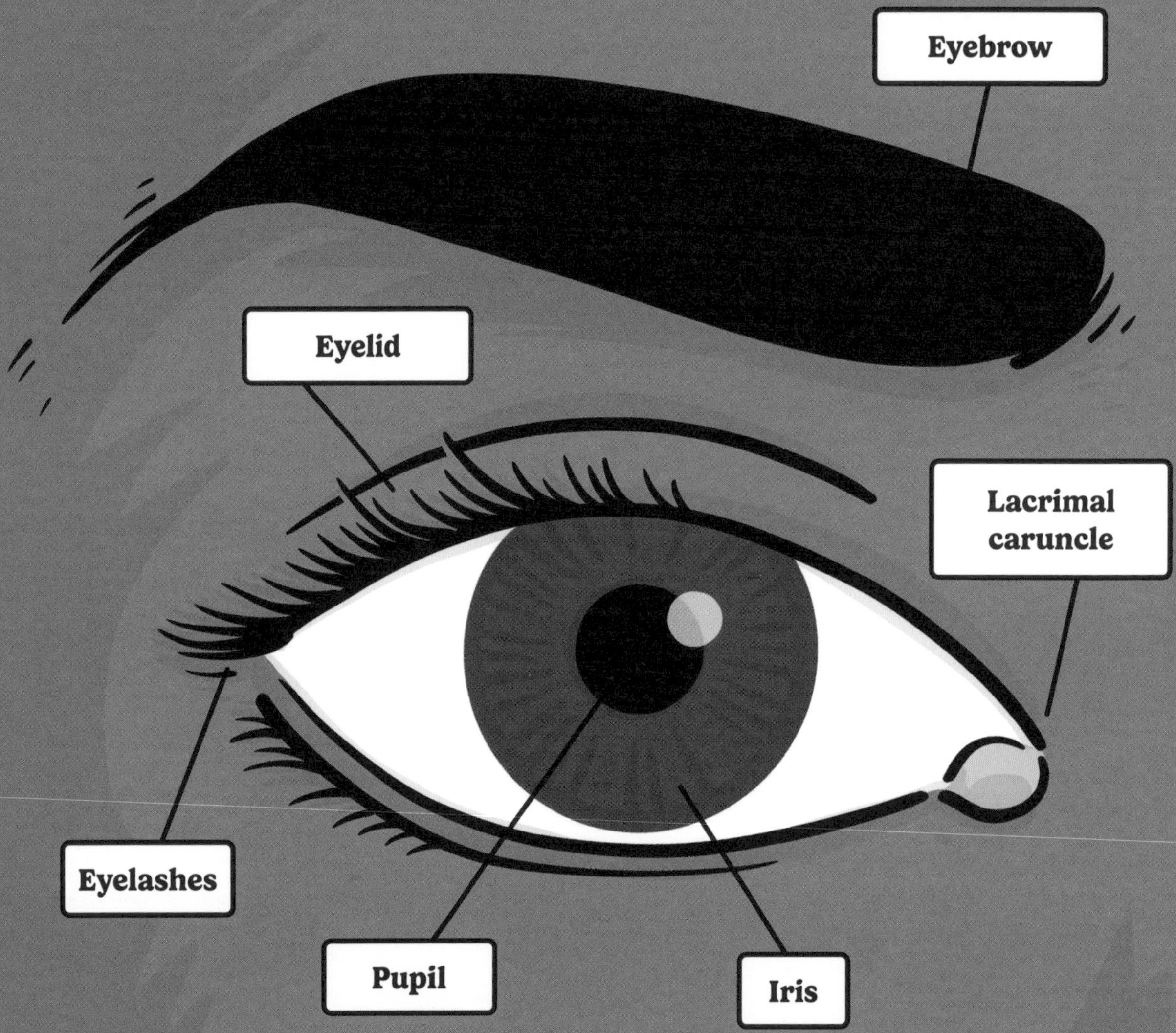

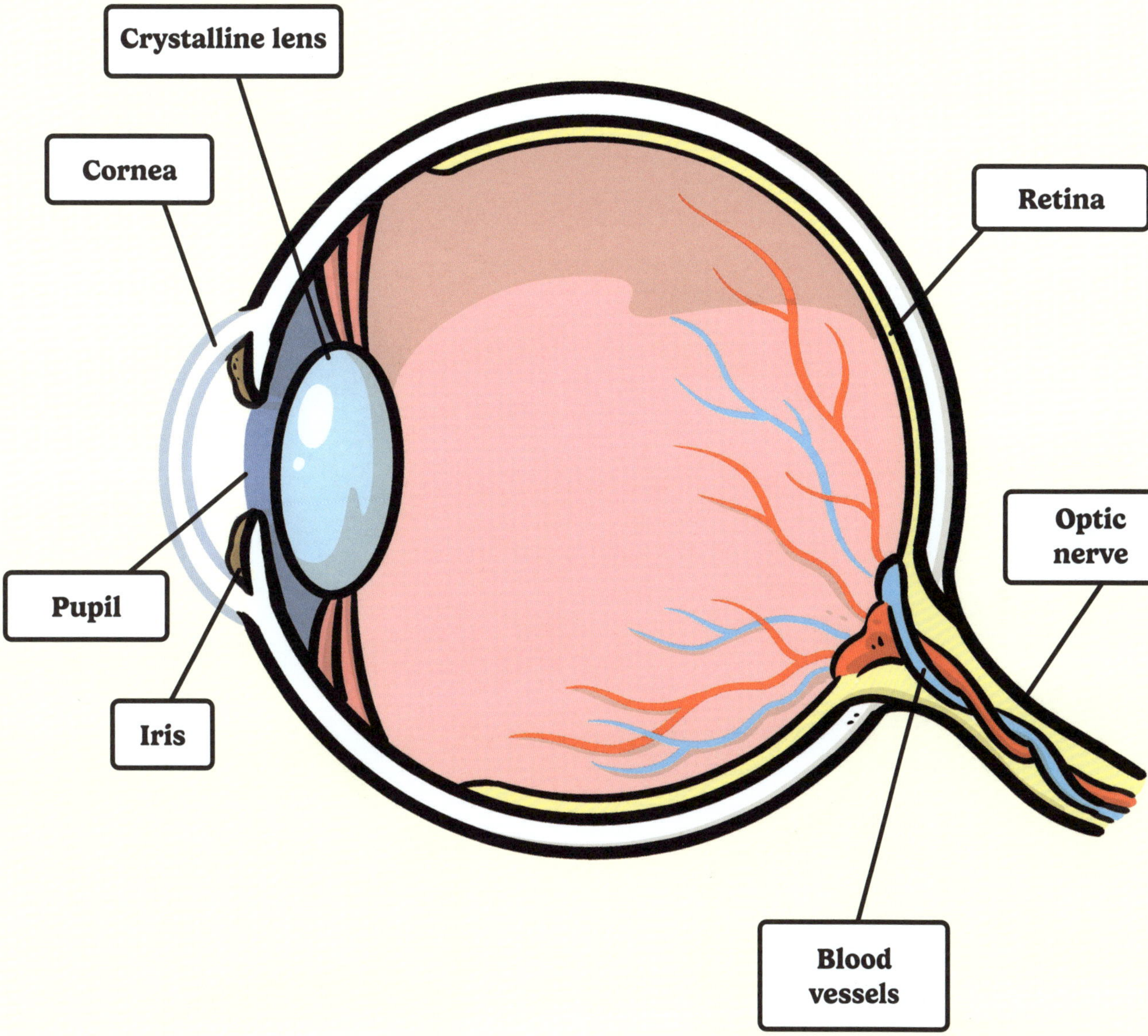
Crystalline lens
Cornea
Retina
Optic nerve
Pupil
Iris
Blood vessels

Tears

The lacrimal glands are located under the lid, above the eye. This is where tears are produced. You cry, don't you? Me too! Have you ever noticed there are two types of tears? There are the tears that flow as a reaction to things like wind or onions. And then there are those that come as an emotional response to sadness, joy, or upsetting news. All tears are very salty, and it is estimated that our eyes can produce up to 100 quarts in a lifetime!

Eyelids

We have eyelids to shield our eyes from wind, dust, or overly bright light. Eyelids act like little windshield wipers, spreading tears over the cornea to keep it moist.

Eyes can be black, green, brown, blue, or beige. Some people even have heterochromia! Heterochromia? That's when a person's eyes have different-colored irises, or when a single iris has more than one color. Eyes can also be round, almond-shaped, big, small ...

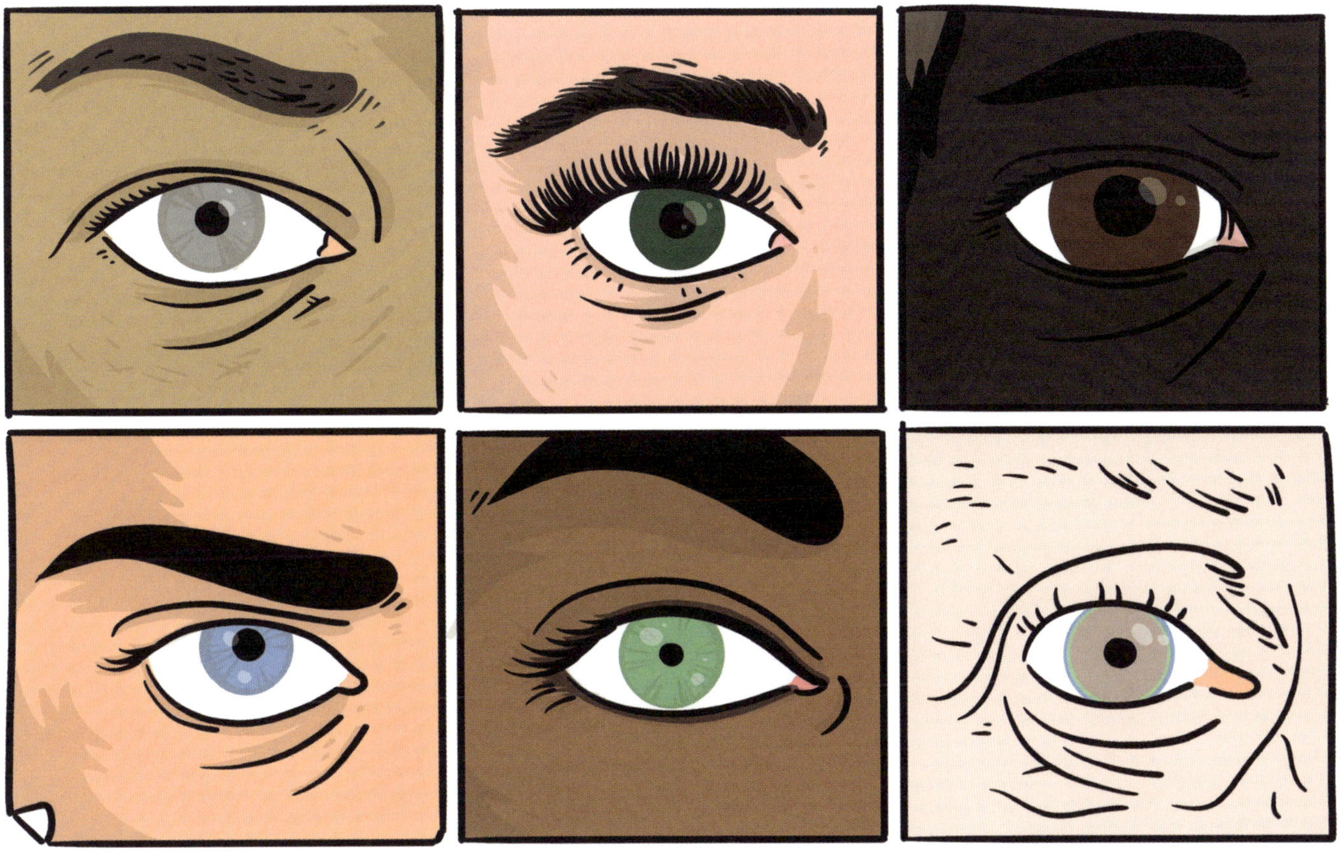

What do your eyes look like?

Sight—How it Works

When you open your eyes and see an **object ❶**, the light that reflects off it enters your eye through an opening called the **pupil**.

The **iris ❷** controls the size of that opening, thus determining the amount of light that enters your eye. If there's too much, you can damage your eye; if there's not enough, you won't see much at all, like trying to see in the dark.

The light that reflects off your object is then focused on a sort of magnifying glass inside your eye. That's the **crystalline lens ❸**, and it creates an image. Just like a camera, it controls how sharp the image is by stretching to see things that are far and contracting to see things that are close. If the lens does its job, the clear image is projected onto the retina upside down.

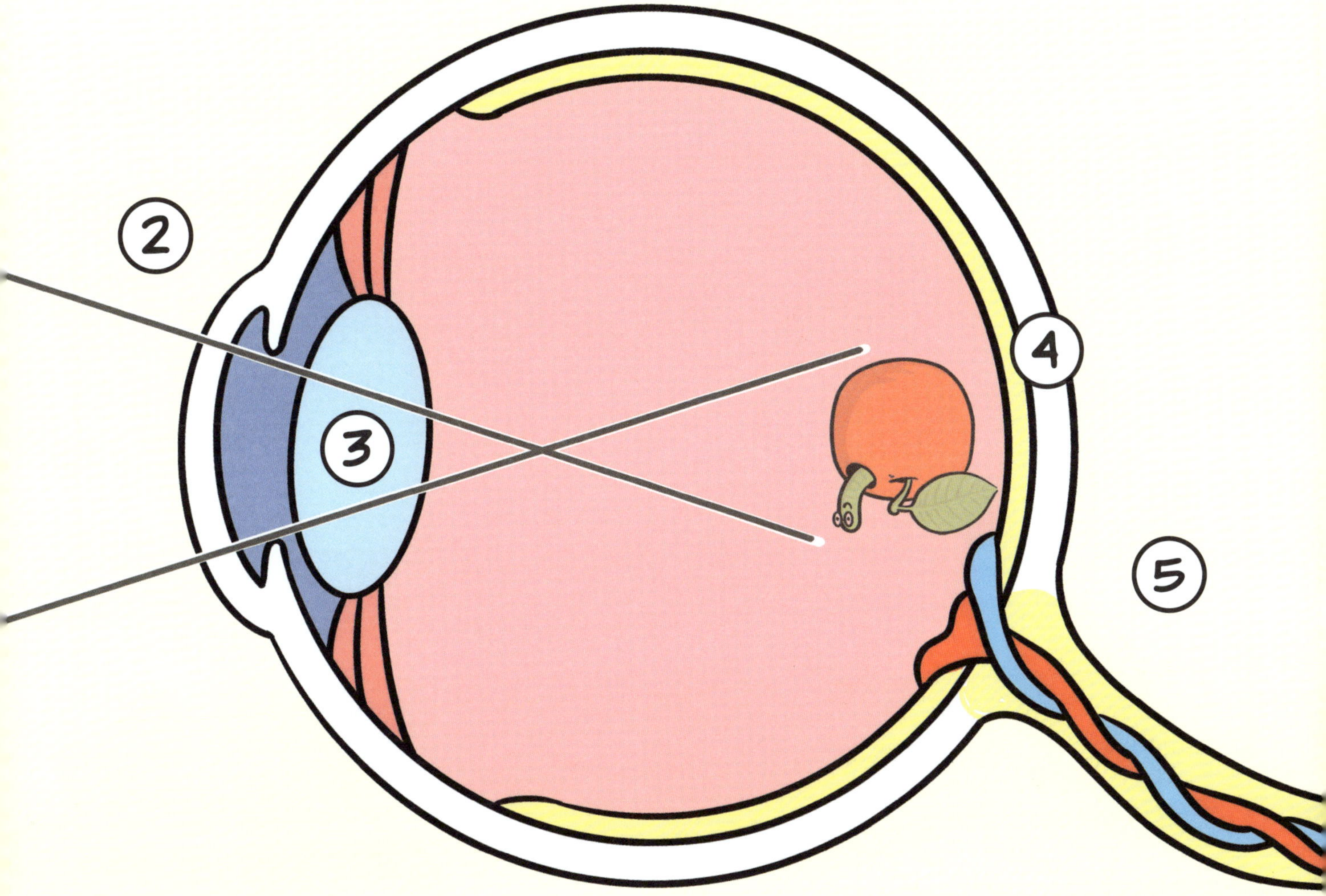

Why is the image upside down? Well, it's because the crystalline lens is curved, not straight, so the light rays that hit it on the bottom are reflected upward, and vice versa.

The **brain** then "translates" these impulses, turning the object right side up.

As for the **retina** ❹, it's a tiny screen capable of differentiating hundreds of color shades and more than 750 degrees of brightness. The retina converts these light rays into electric impulses that are sent to the brain through the **optic nerve** ❺.

Seeing in 3D

You can thank both your eyes for the ability to see so well and perceive depth. Each eye sees the object or scene you're looking at in a slightly different way. The brain then combines the two images, giving three-dimensional, or 3D, vision.

How about a little experiment?

Close one eye and ask someone to hold up a small object, a pencil for instance, about one arm's length in front of you. Try to touch it with a finger. Now try that again with both eyes open. See the difference?

Seeing in Color

Light isn't white; rather, it's made up of all the colors of the rainbow. When light hits an object, the object absorbs some of the colors and reflects the rest. For example, a tennis ball is yellow because it keeps all the other colors and only reflects yellow. And tree leaves are green because they absorb all colors but green. Got it?

Myopia
(Nearsightedness)

Myopia means nearsightedness. A nearsighted person sees close objects well but distant objects poorly. This is because the image is created in front of the retina instead of on the retina, and it can happen when the eye is too long, or the cornea too curved.

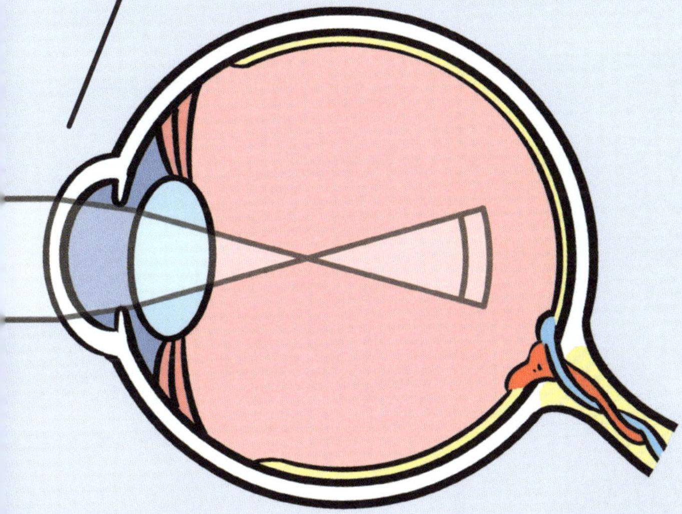

Nearsighted people wear glasses with lenses that are concave, or "hollowed out"—that is, thin in the center but thick at the edge. This diverges light rays so that the image is projected perfectly onto the retina.

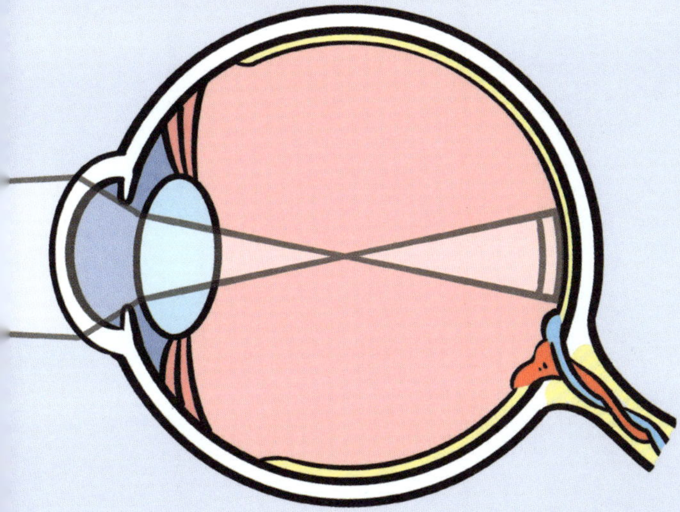

As you read at the beginning of this book, a vast number of people in the world are nearsighted, and increasingly so. To keep from becoming nearsighted, or to keep your nearsightedness in check, specialists recommend not spending too much time in front of a screen and taking breaks—every 20 minutes, look at something 20 feet away for 20 seconds. They also suggest spending an hour or two outside every day so your eyes can focus on things in the distance. Which is cool because you'll get to see birds, people, or even cars! And don't forget to blink to keep your eyes nice and moist.

One more thing—did you know carrots, spinach, blueberries, and almonds all contain vitamins that can reduce the risk of some eye diseases? Count your lucky stars, because in Roman times, a scientist named Pliny the Elder recommended an eye ointment made from the ashes of rat heads or rat tails mixed with honey, or even rubbing your eyes with an old snakeskin!

Hypermetropia
(Farsightedness)

People with hypermetropia have bad far vision but even worse near vision. The image lands behind the retina when the cornea is too flat, the eyeball too short, or the crystalline lens too weak.

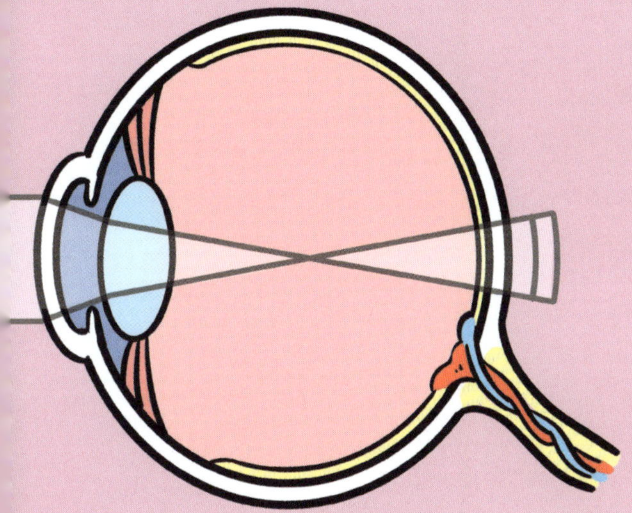

A convex, or outward-bulging, lens is used to converge light rays, causing them to land directly on the retina.

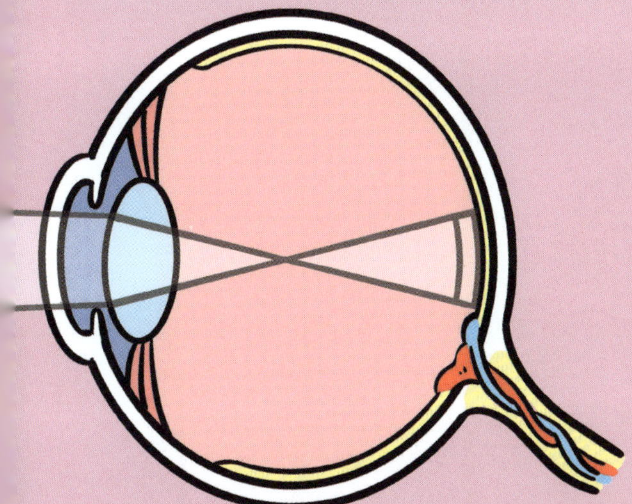

Presbyopia (Age-related vision loss)

This condition affects people as they age. The crystalline lens becomes tired, and it can no longer contract to see close objects, especially when they're small. In other words, you see distant objects better, whereas reading tiny lettering, like the list of ingredients on a package of cookies, is a nightmare!

Presbyopia, or age-related farsightedness, can be corrected with what are called "progressive" lenses, which include a correction for far vision in the center and one for near vision at the bottom.

Astigmatism

With astigmatism, the cornea is oval, not round, which causes images to be distorted. People with astigmatism see poorly regardless of distance.

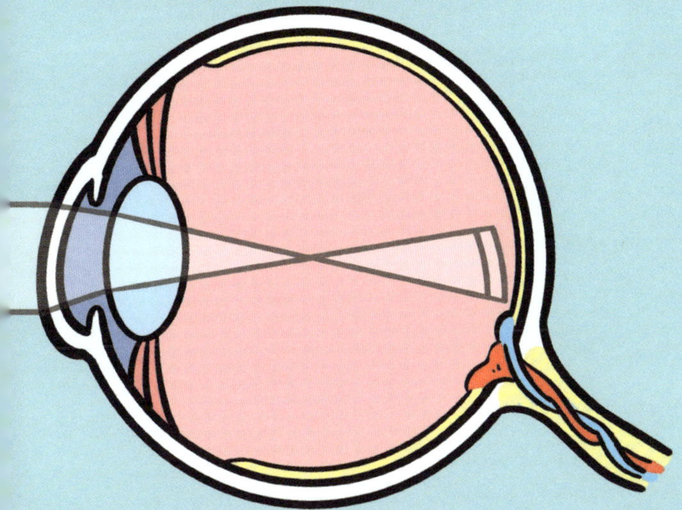

It requires a lens that is cylindrical, domed, and thicker on the sides. This way, it makes up for the uneven shape of the cornea and can adjust sight alignment.

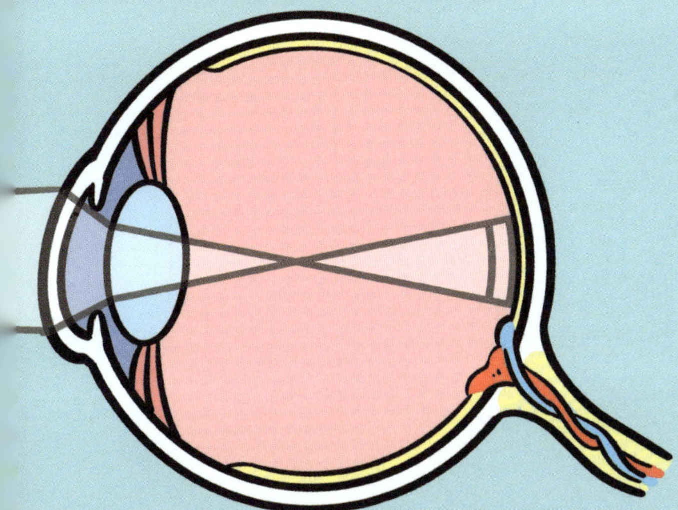

Have you ever noticed that your pupils are not the same size at night as they are in broad daylight? They get bigger in the dark to let in more light.

Look at your pupils in a mirror. Then go spend a few minutes in the dark and come back to the mirror ... do you see how much bigger they are?

Color Blindness

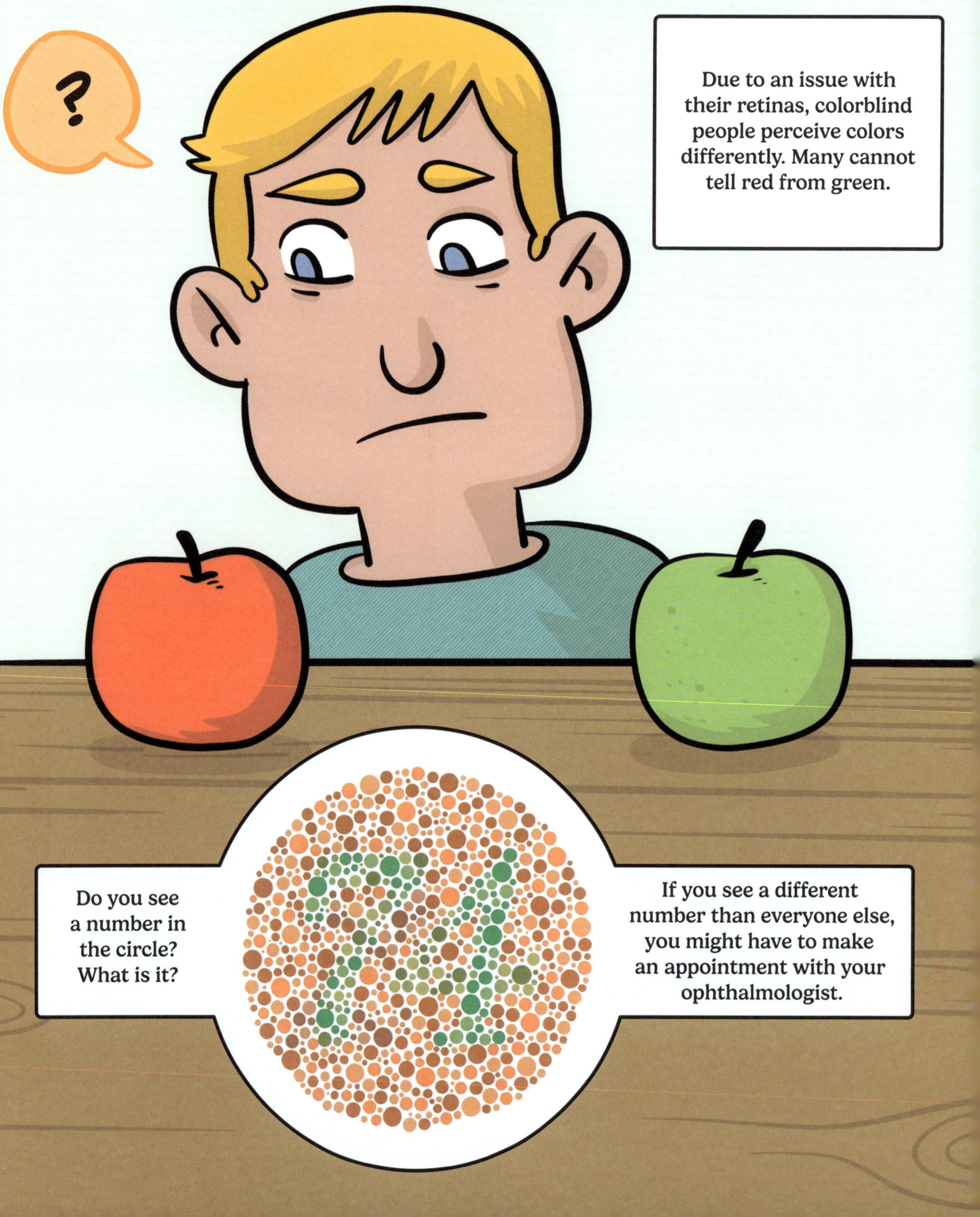

Strabismus

(Sometimes called "crossed eyes" or "lazy eyes")

This is a disorder where the eyes do not properly align, and it can occur when one eye does not function as well as the other. The misaligned eye does not see as well; it is said to be "lazy" or "crossed" and turns outward or inward from its axis. The condition may be corrected by placing a bandage over the strong eye to force the weak one to work harder. Surgery is also an option.

Blindness

Unfortunately, sometimes a person's vision is so bad there are no glasses capable of giving them their sight back. Some people are not able to see anything at all.

These people naturally focus much more on sounds, and some learn to "see" with their hands. Many use a white mobility cane to get around, and some rely on specially trained dogs.

To read, people with strong visual impairments move their fingers over the raised letters of the braille alphabet, named for Frenchman Louis Braille who invented it in the 19th century.
CAN YOU DECIPHER THIS MESSAGE?
*The translation can be found at the end of the book, where there is also a link to a printout.
a b c d e f g h i j
k l m n o p q r s t
u v w x y z : , ‘ .

Why Wear Glasses?

At the Ophthalmologist's

This helps figure out if you are nearsighted or farsighted, or if you have an astigmatism. Then, you'll be asked to read letters or drawings that get smaller and smaller to determine the type of glasses you'll need.
And then, if necessary, you'll go see an optician to buy a pair of glasses or contact lenses.

At the Factory and the Optician's

Do you know how glasses are made? Metal frames are made from metal wire that is twisted and soldered to give them their shape. For plastic frames, the plastic is colored and then molded. Some frames are made from recycled plastic bottles or fishing nets.

What about lenses? In the past, lenses were glass, which is why we call them "glasses." Today, however, most lenses are made from plastic. In a factory, they are poured into small, round molds or cut right from a sheet. Then the lenses are polished to make them see-through. Next, they're sculpted and contoured into the exact shape required for the eyesight of the person who'll be wearing them. Different treatments are applied, like a thin coating to protect against the sun or scratches. The last step in the process is where the optician trims the lenses, so they fit into the frames you picked out.

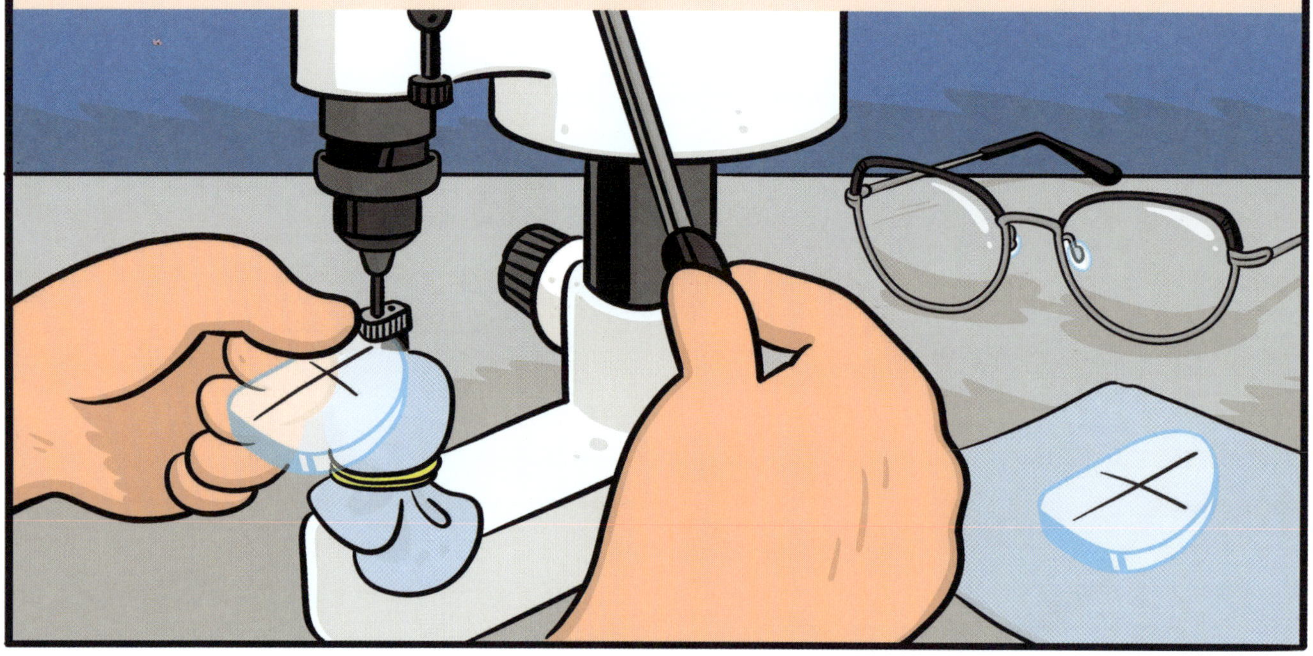

See page 79 for a link to
a printable worksheet.

Eyeglass Parts

Can you name the different parts?

1. Temple
2. Hinge
3. Lens
4. Rim
5. Temple tip
6. Bridge
7. Frame
8. Nose pads

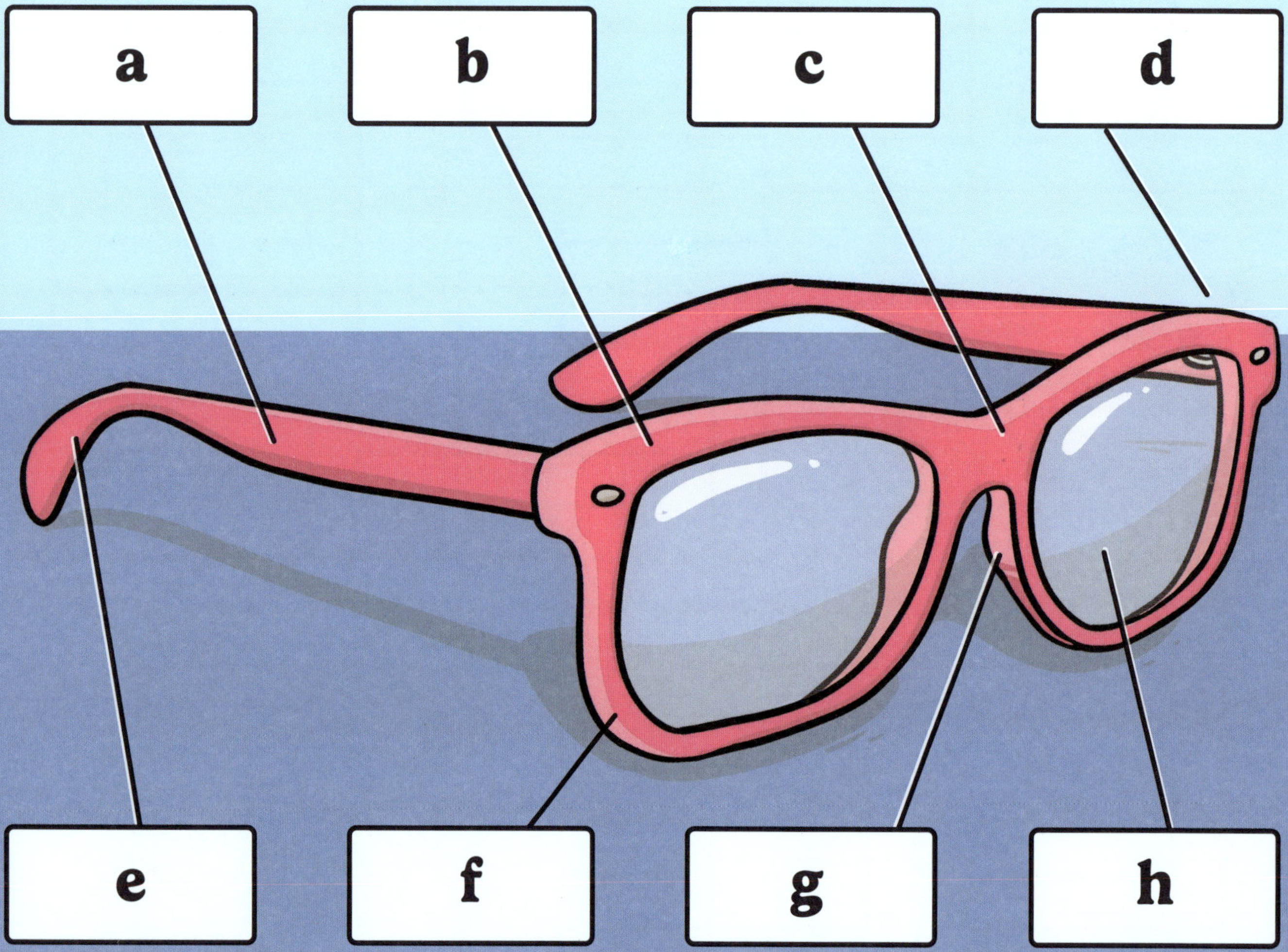

*See page 78 for the answers.

Pluses and Minuses

Do you know what a **diopter** is? It's not another vision disorder; it's a unit for measuring the power of a lens. The higher the diopter, the greater the correction required.

A minus sign (-) in front of a diopter means a person has myopia, while a plus sign (+) indicates a person has hypermetropia. As for the number itself, it indicates the focal length, that is, the distance at which an object comes into focus.

For example, a correction of
-1 means a person without glasses can see objects very well a meter away.
-2 means the focal length is 1 meter divided by 2, or 50 cm.
-4 means the focal length is 1 meter divided by 4, or 25 cm. Got it?

As for far vision, it is measured in tenths. It is believed that newborns have a measurement of 1/10. Older adults are between 5/10 and 7/10, while young adults can even surpass 10/10.

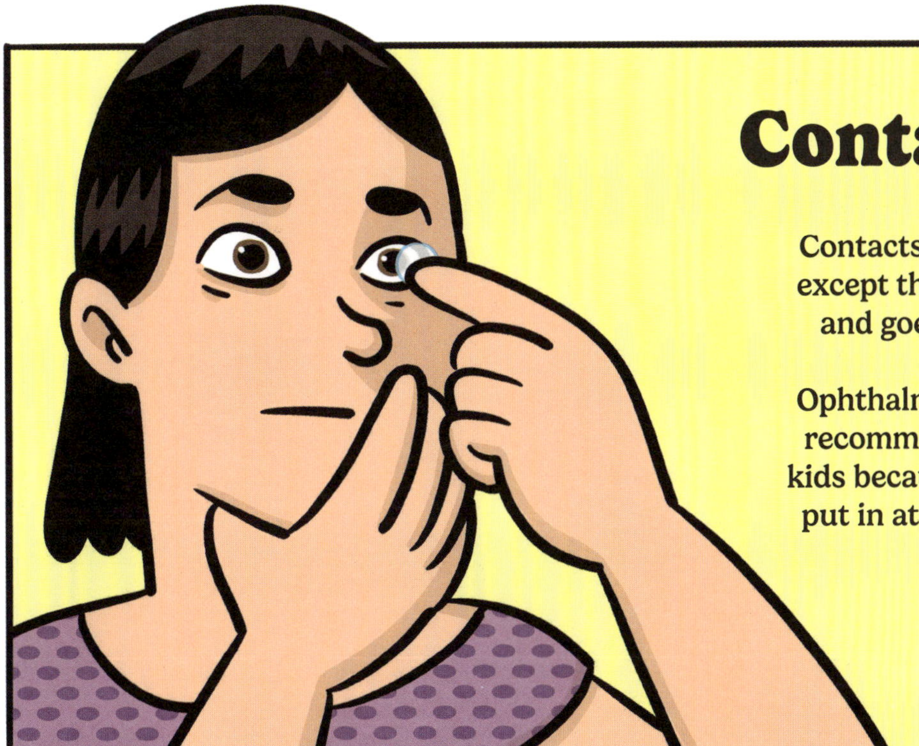

Contact Lenses

Contacts work just like glasses except that the lens is very tiny and goes directly on the eye.

Ophthalmologists usually don't recommend contact lenses for kids because they can be hard to put in at the beginning, among other things.

Handle with Care

Keep Them Clean

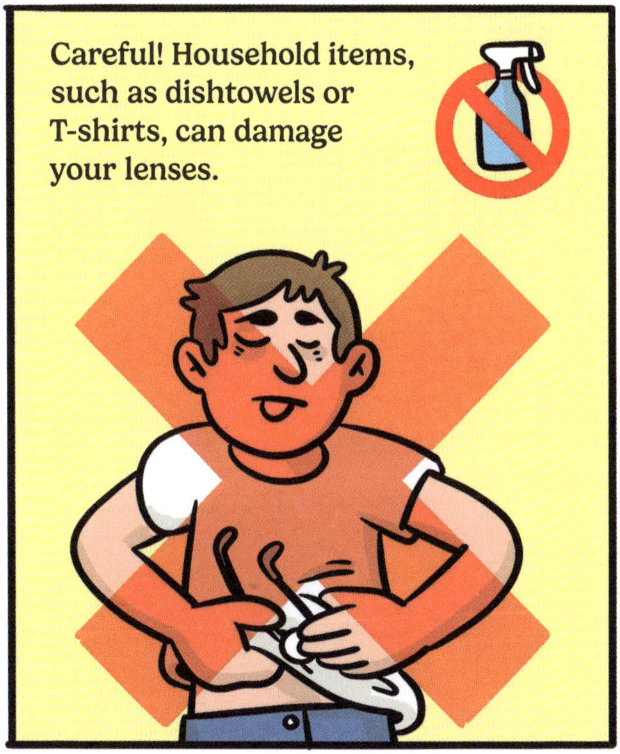

Find the Seven Differences

Eyewear

Beryl
and the Superpowered Spectacles

AAAAAAAA
!
EEEEEEEEE
?
?
?
?
EEEEEEE
END

Glasses for Work

and for Play!

Skiing
Never heard of snow blindness?
Then turn the page.

Swimming
or splashing around
in the water.

Diving
So you can open your
eyes and admire the
underwater scenery.

Sunglasses

While the main purpose of glasses is to improve vision, there are also glasses that offer protection from the sun. You read earlier that colored stones were used in ancient times to keep the sun out of our eyes. In the 18th century, Englishman James Ayscough equipped a frame with tinted lenses for medical reasons.

But it was in the 20th century that sunglasses really took off. They were first developed for pilots in Italy during World War I. Flying high in the sky, pilots were often bothered by the brightness of the sun and its ultraviolet rays. Yet, they had to keep their eyes open. Soon after, sunglasses became popular among race car drivers, too.

In the 1930s, the United States began to mass-produce colored lenses and sunglasses became much more affordable. Hollywood stars began to sport them in the 1950s to keep from being recognized, or the opposite—to stand out.

That radically changed how people saw glasses, which became a cool and stylish accessory.

and Snow Glasses!

Whether you're on the ski slopes or out on the ice floes, you need protection. All that ice and those pretty, white flakes do a terrific job of reflecting the sun's rays, which can be pretty hard on the eyes. In the mountains, where there are more ultraviolet rays than at lower altitudes, you're even likely to become "snow blind" if you're not wearing any protection.

To protect themselves from the blinding Arctic glare, the Inuit invented **snow glasses with very narrow slits**.

In the Eyeglass Family

The **microscope**, for studying microbes, or very tiny organisms
HELLO!
Binoculars, for animal watching and spying on the neighbors

Magnifying Glasses

And what about magnifying glasses? Grandparents and investigators use these instruments to make things bigger.

When you put a magnifying glass in front of your eye, it changes the trajectory of the light rays projected onto the retina, which makes the object appear larger.

What is in the leaves? Connect the dots to find out!

See page 79 for a link to a printable worksheet.

Beryl
and the Superpowered Spectacles
!

SNIFF SNIFF
?
BRR
WAH!
SNIFF
!
?
END

Glasses and Art

Painters have been painting glasses since the time they were invented, as you saw in the piece on page 9 or in **this portrait of Saint Peter** painted by Friedrich Herlin in 1466.

Much later, glasses made their appearance in contemporary art—with surprising twists! In 1937, for example, Marcel Mariën designed glasses for a one-eyed cyclops. In 2013, Mayura Torii and Nicolas Grimmer created a pair of glasses for lovers.

What do you think they looked like? Would you like to draw them? What are the strangest glasses you can imagine?

3D Glasses

But glasses can also help you better enjoy certain works of art. For example, you'll need special glasses if you want to appreciate 3D photographs, films, or even comic strips. The word for this is "stereoscopy" and its invention dates to the 19th century. The most common design is a frame with plastic lenses—one red and one blue—and if you use one, the image below will be sharper and three-dimensional.

Remember, it's because we have two slightly spaced eyes that we can see depth. The brain reconstructs a 3D image by combining what each eye sees. Here, it's basically the same process: the picture is made up of two slightly staggered, identical images. The glasses allow one image to enter one eye and the other image to enter the other eye. Basically, each eye is feeding a separate message to the brain, which interprets them as one image with several dimensions.

Glasses of the Future

With augmented reality, you can even take a walk inside a piece of art or a movie. Have you ever visited a museum or a cathedral in the comfort of your own living room simply by donning a headset or special glasses? There are even glasses that play music through the temples or that are capable of filming. What will the glasses of tomorrow be able to do?

Thanks to artificial intelligence, smart glasses will be able to anticipate our needs. For example, they'll be able to display your shopping list when you're at the store, because your smart refrigerator will have told your glasses you're out of milk or broccoli. Not a fan of broccoli? Too bad, because your glasses will also tell you that the package of cookies you're eyeing contains far too much sugar!

They'll also give you directions when you're trying to get somewhere, just like GPS and smart phones do today, only you won't have to prompt it. Glasses will also be able to read lips, translate live conversations, and tell you all about the monument you're looking at. So, if you're strolling through Paris and gaze up at the Eiffel Tower, a text or a voice will teach you that it was finished in 1889, is made up of 18,038 pieces of metal, and is nearly 1,110 feet (330 meters) tall.

Glasses and Stereotypes

In addition to the glasses of the future, there are also the glasses of the past. When your grandparents or parents were small, it wasn't always easy to wear glasses. They weren't all that common and they weren't very attractive, and so they often led to teasing. Kids were called geeks or four-eyes. People who wear glasses are often considered "nerds"—and nerdy characters in books, movies, and cartoons are often spectacled. That's because for a very long time, eyeglasses were an accessory available only to those who knew how to read and write. And those people were usually men, because education was a male-dominated privilege.

Have you ever been teased? And what's wrong with being intelligent, anyway? Remember, glasses are jam-packed with superpowers!

How About Animals?

Flies have huge eyes that allow them to see 360° and 200 frames, or movements, per second, compared to only 24 for humans. That's why they're so hard to catch!

Cats are slightly nearsighted, but they see much better in the dark than we do thanks to more light sensors in the retina, a reflective coating over the eye, and pupils that can open very wide (which also makes them very cute).

Have you ever noticed that **goats** and **sheep** have perfectly rectangular pupils? This enables them to see what's behind them without having to turn their head. So, they can graze away in peace and still watch out for predators.
!

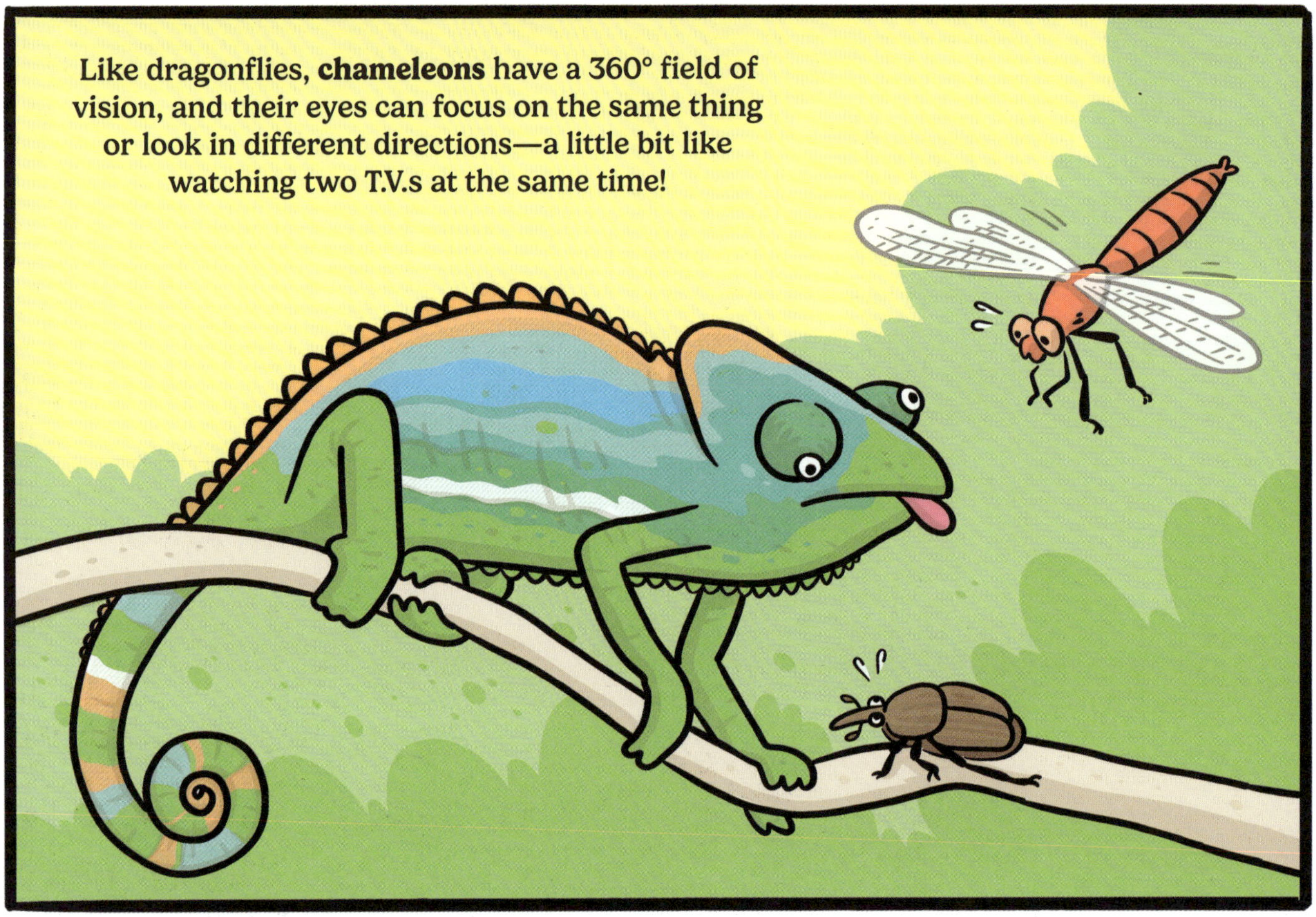
Like dragonflies, **chameleons** have a 360° field of vision, and their eyes can focus on the same thing or look in different directions—a little bit like watching two T.V.s at the same time!

One little crustacean found in the Pacific and Indian oceans is the owner of the most complex eyes in the entire animal kingdom. Like a chameleon, the **mantis shrimp** can turn its eyes in every direction. And like some birds, it can see ultraviolet light. Each eye is equipped with millions of photoreceptors and capable of making whatever adjustments are necessary to better see what it's looking at. But we still have no idea why it needs all that at the bottom of the ocean!

Birds of prey like falcons, eagles, and owls can see over incredible distances. The red-tailed hawk can detect a mouse moving from 100 feet away!
10 tiny rodents are hiding in this picture. Can you spot them?

Spectacled Animals

Spectacled owl

Spectacled bear

Panda
According to a Tibetan legend, after their baby sister disappeared, pandas began to cry and used their black paws to wipe away the tears. The rubbing left a mark. Scientists think that the rings around their eyes allow pandas to tell each other apart.

Spectacled, or Indian, cobra
According to an Indian tale, the god Shiva gave this snake two spots that look like eyeglasses as a thank-you for sheltering him from the sun. But zoologists believe the spectacled cobra has these spots, called a hood mark, to scare predators.

Beryl
and the Superpowered Spectacles

MEOW!
?
MEOW!
??
?
END

Optical Illusions

These are images that use certain colors and shapes to trick our eyes and our brains. We think we see something, but it's just an illusion. And there are no glasses to help with that!

Here, for example, you see the image moving, right? But how can it move when it's printed on the page of a book? The truth is your eye is doing the moving and that's because it doesn't know where to rest.
Which line is longer? What if I told you they are exactly the same length? It's because of the arrows that one seems to be longer than the other.
The same goes for these two monsters, which are actually the same size! It's the effect of perspective—we know that things that are farther from us should be smaller. Try this experiment: stand in front of your house or building and look at it. Then look at it from across the street.

Quiz

1.

What did emperor Nero use for sunglasses?

A. A green stone

B. A saucepan

C. A piece of plastic

2.

Another word for glasses is

A. Spectrums

B. Spectacles

C. Spectroscopes

3.

Myopia is

A. When you cannot see things close-up

B. When you cannot see things far away

C. When you cannot perceive depth

4.

A telescope is for

A. Watching T.V.

B. Teleporting yourself

C. Stargazing

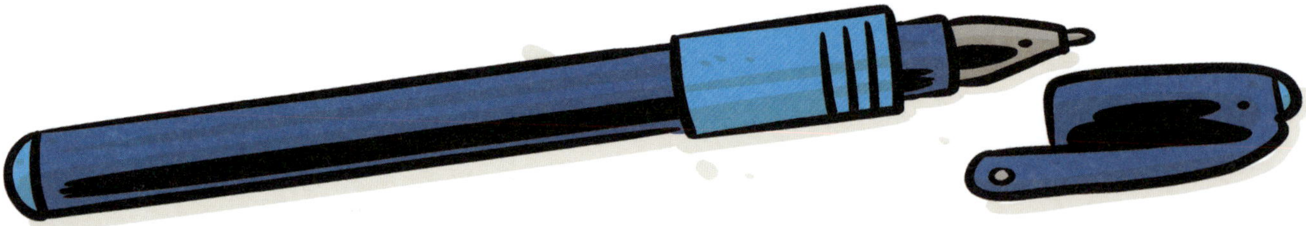

5.

Color blindness is when you

A. Are blinded by bright colors

B. Have trouble differentiating colors

C. Prefer yellow to red

6.

Contact lenses are

A. An Indian dish

B. Tiny disks that sit directly on your eyes

C. A muscle in the eyelid

7.

Heterochromia is when you have eyes that are

A. Different colors

B. Green and brown

C. Identical

8.

Pandas have black rings around their eyes because

A. They are fans of the band, The Cure

B. That's how they identify one another

C. They rubbed their eyes without washing their paws

9.

Cats can see

A. 360 °

B. At night

C. Mice from 2 miles away

10.

The lenses of most modern glasses are made

A. From glass

B. From plastic

C. In China

Answer Key

JUST BECAUSE A MAN LACKS THE USE OF HIS EYES DOESN'T MEAN HE LACKS VISION.

STEVIE WONDER

(American singer-songwriter born in 1950)

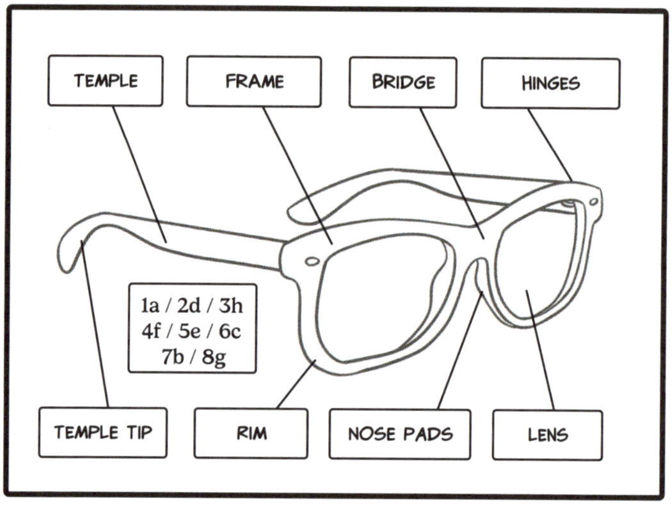

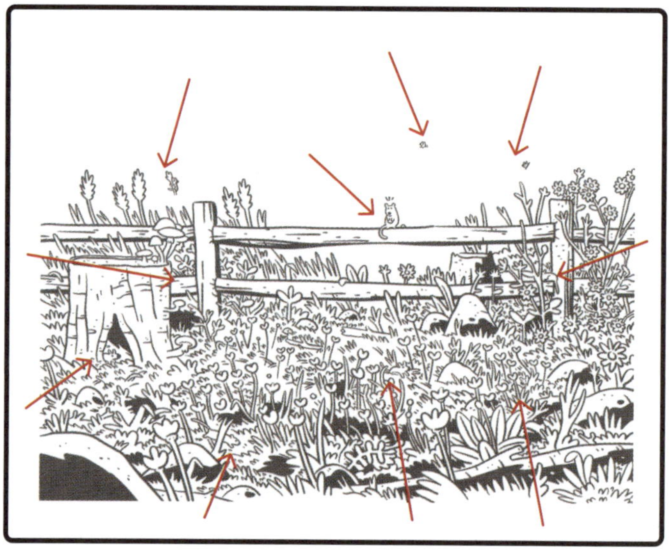

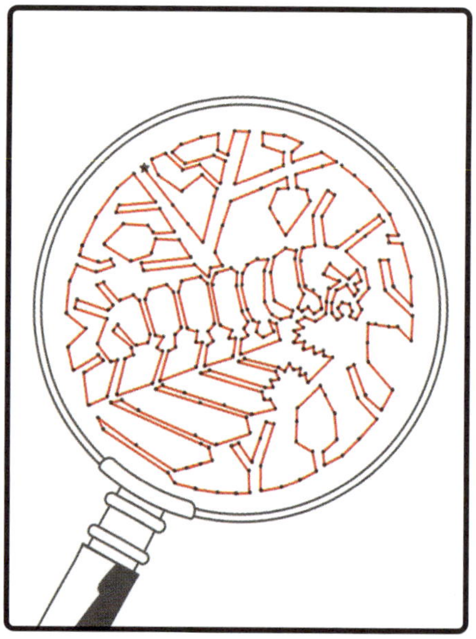

Quiz Answers:
1. A / 2. B / 3. B / 4. C
5. B / 6. B / 7. A / 8. B
9. B / 10. B+C

Did you recognize the hidden celebrities on pages 14 and 15? Mahatma Gandhi, Malcom X, Marylin Monroe, Le Corbusier, Elton John, Audrey Hepburn, John Lennon, and Iris Apfel.

Educators' Resources

How does the story of eyeglasses help *everyone* see the world clearly? Reflect, experiment, and explore to find out!

Reflect

Look at the illustration on pages 14 and 15. There are so many ways that eyeglasses express the individuality of the wearer; there are as many possibilities as there are people. Design your own frames to reflect who you are. What colors, patterns, and shapes will your design include?

In addition to our specific eye structures, our brains also use memories, emotions, and knowledge to shape our perspectives about the things we see. Look at a painting with a friend or small group. Write your own lists of five things in the painting that you notice right away. Take turns sharing your writing. What did your perspectives have in common? What was different?

Experiment

Before the invention of shaped lenses, people used dishes of water or cut gems to magnify print. What was that like? Fill a clear dish or glass with water. Place a piece of paper with words printed on it on a table. Look at the words through the bottom of the dish or glass. Then look at the same words through a magnifying glass. Try this with different sizes of text. Record your observations and ideas.

Take a close look at the eyeball diagram on pages 24 and 25. Use spoons to get a sense of how the shape of eyes, corneas, and lenses impact how we see. What do you notice when you look at your reflection on the convex side of the spoon? What about the concave side? What happens to your reflection when you use a round spoon or oval spoon?

Explore

Eyeglasses have changed a lot since in the 13th century! On page 42, the author describes some different materials used to make modern eyeglass frames, including metal, recycled plastic bottles, and fishing nets. What else can be used to make eyeglass frames? Research companies using innovative and sustainable materials to learn more about the evolution of eyeglass design and technology.

Today, many people all over the world need glasses but are not able to afford them. What is being done today to help people who need vision support? How can you help organizations trying to provide access to eyeglasses?

Get your printable worksheets here!
https://hello.helvetiq.com/eyeglasses

Caroline Stevan has been wearing glasses since she was just two years old. Wearing glasses has helped her write numerous articles for the newspaper, *Le Temps*, and produce many episodes of *Point J*, a current affairs podcast for RSR (*Radio Suisse Romande*), where she still works today. This book is her fourth for Helvetiq.

She would like to thank Salomé and her little blue glasses, her inspiration for this book, as well as Aude and Hadi for their support and belief, François for his artwork and energy, Anissa for checking the science, and the Visilab Pully team for teaching her about vision.

François Vigneault is a cartoonist and illustrator. He is the co-creator of the YA graphic novel *13e Avenue* published by Éditions de la Pastèque in 2018 and the comic book series *Orcs in Space* from Oni Press (2021–22). His relatively small body of work has been nominated for a surprising number of awards (including the Joe Shuster Award and the Bédélys Québec Award) and has even won a few of them, including the inaugural Québec Bookseller's Prize for best youth graphic novel. Born in the United States to Haitian and French-Canadian parents, he grew up in San Diego, California and lived in San Francisco and Portland, Oregon before landing in Quebec in 2015, where he has lived ever since.